# Naked
# Screaming

K. J. Sharpe

In Memory of My Firstborn

Robert Alan Powell II

Never Forgotten. Always on my mind.

*-Muddah*

# CONTENTS

# ACKNOWLEDGMENTS

I am always grateful to the plethora of people who help make my work possible simply by sharing life with them. Special thanks to my multitalented eldest daughter, Nicole Morain, who is both the model and photographer for the cover photo that captures the heart and soul of this work.

Special thanks also to my youngest son, Robby Atkins, for producing the photograph of his older brother, Robert Alan Powell II. A talented artist and wordsmith in his own right, Robby continues to inspire me to do more.

Thank you to all my children, grandchildren, family, and friends for your encouragement as I continue to share my work. Thank you for caring for and supporting me in so many ways when I couldn't care for myself. Thank you for helping me to maintain my sanity in a world gone crazy. I love you all.

Thanks be to God, truly the love in my life, who always causes me to triumph. No matter how often I stumble and fall or wallow in the mud, he is still with me. I am thankful for meditation, grace, love, mindfulness, and faith that continue to keep me alive and well.

I am grateful for a world in which we may not all agree, but we all have a voice. I am grateful for the calling to effectively and unapologetically use mine.

# CHAPTER ONE

# IDENTITY

Step into the water my friend
In its quiet
And its rushing
If you listen
It will tell you who you really are.

# NAKED SCREAMING

I would like to be running down the beach right now

Naked

And screaming

Do you think anyone would mind?

Just this one time?

If I disrobe

Unclothe myself of the weight

Of all my responsibilities

All the tasks to be done in a timely manner

Lay them out on the shore

To be swallowed by the sand and the sea

Muddied and drifting away in tides that know no time

If I could just run

On the beach

Making footprints in the sand

Naked

And screaming.

# THE WAY HOME

Come with me and I will tell you about life.

The glaring truth of it.

The horrible pain and tremendous joy of it.

It's empty, hollow powerlessness

And the human will's

Determined, remarkable strength.


Come with me and I will share the tales

Like Anansi and Coyote stories of old

I'll tell you about falling

Hard

And rising from the ashes, dirt, and mud

Bruised, battered, and broken

But standing tall inside yourself.


Walk through the abyss with me

Dwell in a darkness so profound

Its blackness swallows your soul

Silent as the grave where you laid your child

      Your fathers

            Your brother

                  Your best friend

Silent and deep

Deeper than the six-foot hole

That leaves a hole

In your whole heart.


I dare you to walk with me

Through the ruins
On paths where there is no light
Where even the spirits cease to dwell
And the "still small voice" no longer whispers
In the utter darkness of hell.

Walk with me through the highs
And lows and in-between times
That changed my life
And altered my light.

Walke with me
And scream your naked
Violent
Grieving
Joyous screams
Walk with me
And find your way
Home.

# I AM A WOMAN

Let me start by saying this:

I am a woman.
I was born female with all the body parts and potential
Of womanhood.

I Am A Woman
Not only because I have grown other human beings
Cradled in my body
Moving my muscles, bones, and organs out of place
To give birth
And feed them
Naturally
From my swollen
Aching breasts
Filled with the milk of life
Colostrum
Nutrients that fed
Their present and future

I AM A Woman
I know how to bear down and take the pain

Because I was born for it
And so
I have endured rejection
And being discounted
I have weathered the storms of ignorance
And bloodied words
And tolerated the pain of blame
When insecure men
Have called me out of my name
Cause they couldn't run game
I bore the shame
Of rape and ridicule
Being called a bitch
For standing up for who I am
And what I was born to do.

I AM A WOMAN.
Not only because I have a vagina that bleeds

And an entire circuitry of hormones
And chemistry
That can kill 2.5 million sperm
Racing to the promised land
To procreate inside of me

I am a superbly powerful human being
And on the battlefield between my legs
Men have cum to live
And die
Worshipping and speaking in tongues
At the altar of my womanness.

I AM A WOMAN!
The giver and sustainer of life
I give birth spiritually
Physically
Mentally
Completely
Naturally
Incubating ideas, concepts, ambitions, thoughts, visions, and dreams
Manifesting them into reality on the earth
And beyond the stars
I am the details of the big picture
Because
I see deeper
My vision intuitive
My comprehension multiplicative
I AM

The algebraic and geometric expression
Of life

I AM A WOMAN.
I am much more than hair and nails
Eyelashes and asses
Expensive
Priceless
I AM
Much more valuable
Than high heels with red bottoms
Matching lipstick shades
I AM
The mystery and history of the universe
Infinitesimally iridescent

I shine
Sparkling like diamonds
Made of the millions of stars
In the sky
Costly
I did not come by this price
Without suffering.

I AM A WOMAN

I Am
A Black woman
I AM
A proud woman
An erudite, influential, intellectual
Woman
A wise woman
A natural woman
Endowed with vision, insight, clarity, and creativity
I see from the front
Excreting from behind
And I do not get the two confused.

I AM A WOMAN
I stand fast in my ability
To plow, plant, water, and grow
Full blooded and bloody
I come once again to this battle for my existence
And for my sisters
Spelled S-I-S
And daughters
And the entire family of humankind
With courage I stand and say

I am she
I am her
Who has fought way too many battles to be me
Here I stand
Once again
At a place where I've rarely been
Politically correct
Boldly
Biologically
Defending what God, Source, the Universe
And genetics

Has made me.
I stand before a generation
That asks for definitions
Signs and symbols
Of what is plain
I have explained
So you fully understand that
Without any proclamations or hidden agendas
Without socio-psychological experiment
I was born a woman
I have one spirit

You may have two
But loving myself as I am
Does not automatically correlate
To me hating or fearing you.

I AM A WOMAN
Who loves my femininity
Who embraces my softness
And my power
My resilience
And my strength
In a society that feels the need
For "terf" wars
This is where I stand.

I AM A WOMAN
Take all of this how you want to
As I know you will
But call me by my name
Cause your C-I-S
"Birthing person"
And "Breeder"
Is all sus to me

I AM A WOMAN
100%
Naturally

# NOTE-2-SELF

I love and adore you
I love how you laugh hard and loud
When you think something's funny
Even when no one is laughing with you.
I love how you embrace joy.

I love when you wake up smiling
And grateful
With a song in your heart
And in your mouth
With God
Glory
And joy on your mind.

I love your peace when it comes in waves
Or drips from the sky
I love how you share yourself with others
Even when it drains you
I love your ability to recover and bring light
Regardless of storms
Oblivious to hurricanes
And volcanic eruptions
That challenge your peace.

I love the way you shine like the sun
And how you stand at the edge of the ocean
Marveling at the sky above and sea below
Dancing, swaying, turning with the tide.

I love that you are still a child

No matter how many years

Etch the corners of your eyes.

I love that you could care less if anyone's looking

I admire your natural curiosity about

Everything.

I enjoy your childlike wonder.


I love you

I love all that is you

I love the tempest that rages against injustice

And ignorance

The way you weep for those in pain

And speak up for those who have no voice.

I love that you command attention

Without a word

Or flamboyant behavior

Your light so shines

Brightening the pathway for others

Even those that hate you.


I love who you are

All that you are

And who and what you are not.

I accept your capricious atmospheric conditions

Your fair weather

Your inclement storms

Rain and hail

Fire and fierceness

Blustery, tempestuous winds

Passion and compassion

Rage and repentance

I love your subtlety

And your words that cut like a knife

Your wit

And charm

The tongue that lashes

And the lips that succor with a kiss.


When I look in the mirror and see you

I can't help but smile

The way you tilt your head

As if you're listening for something

No one else can hear

Engaged in silent conversation

With an unknow entity

I love you

And I find you

Fascinating.

# LOVE LETTER

I am in love with myself

Even when I don't know if I like me

When my hair won't act right

 Or my body is all out of sorts

Varying in shape and size

Fighting with the scale and arguing

With a measuring tape

Even when I'm not beautiful to myself

I still love me

I have learned to love me

More today

Than all my yesterdays

Thinking about all the things

That made me who I am

I decided to tell myself

I love you

Now and forever

I loooove me

Some me.

# THE AWAKENING

I am a creator

    As elusive as the wind

    As fluid as water

    As fleeting as time

    As irrefutable as the universe.

I find myself in the stars

    In rivers

    Oceans

    And deep blue seas.

I sit silently

    Reverently

    At the shores of each new awakening

    Wondering

    Who am I

    And what will I create

    Today.

# FLOWER CHILD

I am a flower child

>Who worships the sun

>And kisses rainbows

>Who lays down beneath the clouds

>Searching out the shape of heaven

>Sensing the glory that shines above the storm

I am a flower child

>Like a wind blowing through the trees

>Heat

>Beating upon your back

>Your brow sweating from my balmy

>Caress.

I am a flower child

>I am the light illuminating the darkness

>Igniting your joy

>Setting fire to laughter, and passion, and freedom

>I dance like the flames

>Entranced by the fire.

I am a flower child.

>Like sun showers in summer

>And the warmth of a fire in winter

>I keep you warm

>And safe

>And happy for a while.

I am a flower child

A nymph

>A little sprite thing

>Stirring your imagination

>Escorting you on trips of pure fantasy

I am the journey

     And all your luggage

     The peace

     And the pilgrimage

I am a flower child.

# LIGHT AND LIFE

Illumination and life

I'll bring to you

But sometimes

I too become the color

Of the darkest hues.

# MAJESTY

Born from the royal fortress

Bathed in a cascading pool of light

I came into being

The citadel and the sanctuary

The shelter and the storm

The lion and lamb

Heavy is the head

That wears the crown

Don't look down

I am the gift of Jehovah

Call me by my name

I am

Her majesty

The queen.

# REFLECTING POOL

I spoke to the little girl in me who missed her daddy desperately

The little girl who sat in windows talking to the sky

Trying to reach heaven and hear her father's voice

I gathered her in my arms to hold her

And heal her from all the yesterdays where she felt

 Unseen

 Unheard

 Invisible

I knelt before her tiny frame and spoke to her in soft tones

Enveloping her to myself

I whispered

 You are safe

 You are loved

 You are valuable

 You are worthy

 It's not your fault your daddy's gone

 He didn't desert you

 He adored you

 He loved you too.

I spoke to the little girl inside me to remind me

 You are not alone

 Your father is here with you

 His spirit lives on in you

 You are loved

 You are safe

 You are valuable

 You are beautiful

I held her until we both cried

Me and the little girl inside

I saw her restored and healed.

I watched her grow before my eyes.


I spoke to the young girl inside me

The one who at thirteen

Contemplated her worthlessness and takin her own life

I saw her again

Isolated and alone feeling

      Insignificant

      Unheard

      Invisible

      Worthless

Sadness and grief trailing behind her

Like a snail oozing slime.

How she ran and hid in books

And climbed trees

To get away from the world

Somewhere safe

Gazing, mumbling at the sky

Hidden where no one could see her

And tell her how ugly, unusual, and weird she was.

I reminded her

      I'm here

      You are safe

      You are worthy

      You count

      You are beautiful

      You are loved.

It's not your fault they rejected you

You don't have to accept the names they called you.

> Weird=Unique
>
> Different=Mysterious and Fascinating
>
> Ugly=Creatively designed and exotic
>
> Nerd=Intelligent and inquisitive

I came to put my arms around her

Loved on her

To remind her

> You are safe
>
> You are beautiful
>
> You are worthy
>
> You are not alone.

I watched her blossom and become a woman

> Perfectionist
>
> People-pleaser
>
> And nurturer
>
> She mothered everyone
>
> Still yearning for love and acceptance
>
> She accepted seconds.

I saw her

Tapped her on her shoulder

And whispered in her ear,

> Remember
>
> You are worthy
>
> You are beautiful
>
> You are beloved
>
> You are valuable
>
> You are love.

Then finally,

One day without notice

I watched

And stood proudly beside her

As she became a queen

Slaying dragons

Becoming fire

Sending demons fleeing

Overcoming death, hell,

And close encounters with the grave.

She became

I became

A warrior.

And stood regally inside myself knowing

    I am worthy

    I am valuable

    I am accepted

    I am the beloved of God

    I am more than enough

Healed and happy little girl

I see you

Standing now inside of me

Perfectly imperfect

Valued, loved and accepted

We are one

    The baby girl who lost her daddy way too soon

    The teenager who tripped over and lost herself

    The wounded woman

    And the warrior she became

I see you now

    The lion

Pressing toward destiny

Knowing

I am worthy

I am the blessing

I am powerful

I am a force

I recognize you now

You are loved

You are valuable

You belong.

# I'M SEXY, FUCK YOU

Bougie bitch

Jezebel

Temptress

Whore

Demon and the devil incarnate

I've been called it all

Mostly behind my back

Or in slick inuendo

Cause my temper is dark blue-black

And ain't nobody tryna deal with all that.

Good Christian sisters

With long skirts

Tight lips

And southern comfort smiles clutch their pearls

And their men

Talkin' bout

Praise the Lord sister

That dress is mighty short

> And tight

> And red

When what they really mean is

> Can you cover up them long strong legs

> So my husband won't look

> Wear your skirt to the ground

> So he won't be tempted to wonder

> Can you tuck in the junk in your trunk

And tone down your smile

> So my man won't be peeping across the aisle

> Can you PLEASE dim your shine

Can you be less amiable, less kind

Cause you're causing our men folk

To act real strange about your flesh

I tried

I really did

I wore the high collars

That strangled my throat and silenced my voice

I tried to choke out me

To pacify you

I tried

I really did

I wore the skirts down to my slender ankles

And the sleeves that hid my tiny wrists

But I learned

That covering up me

Would not heal

Your insecurity

So

Here I stand

And sit

And cross my legs

In all my glory

Saying

I'm sexy

Fuck you.

It ain't my fault you hiding your sexy too.

Wearing grandma drawls

And them white washed usher shoes

That was never meant for you

Smile sometimes

Flip that nasty judgmental, condescending attitude

You mad at me

Cause I know I'm sexy

And I own it

It ain't the clothes that's bothering you

It's the fact that no matter what I wear

I own the room

Cause I'm not ashamed of who I am

Shiiiituh!

I'm sexy

Fuck you.

# WHEN I CUT MY HAIR

Warrior

That's what I am

That's what you can expect from me

When I cut my hair

Don't look for the pretty girl

Cause she's gone

Don't expect me to be nice

Or polite

Or to try NOT to hurt your feelings

I'm at War!

And all's fair

Your feelings no longer matter to me

When I cut my hair.

When I cut my hair

It's kick your ass time

It's watch your back time

It's walk up on you

Grab you by your throat

Whisper

Remember me

While I choke you out time

Cause when I cut my hair

It means I no longer care.

When I cut my hair

And put my war clothes on

Adorned in my sugar and spice camouflage

Nobody knows what to expect

Or what I will do

Won't even know when

Or how

I'm coming for you

Moving stealth

Silent as the grave

Soundless

Up close and personal

Or nowhere around

My sister says I "go dark"

My mother used to say

"She's real nice. Just don't make her mad."

Too bad

So sad

You mad?

Too bad

When I cut my hair

It's a warning

Not a threat

Or some weak ass promise

I'm imparting knowledge

So you know

That when I cut my hair

The time to play fair

Is over.

# CHAPTER TWO

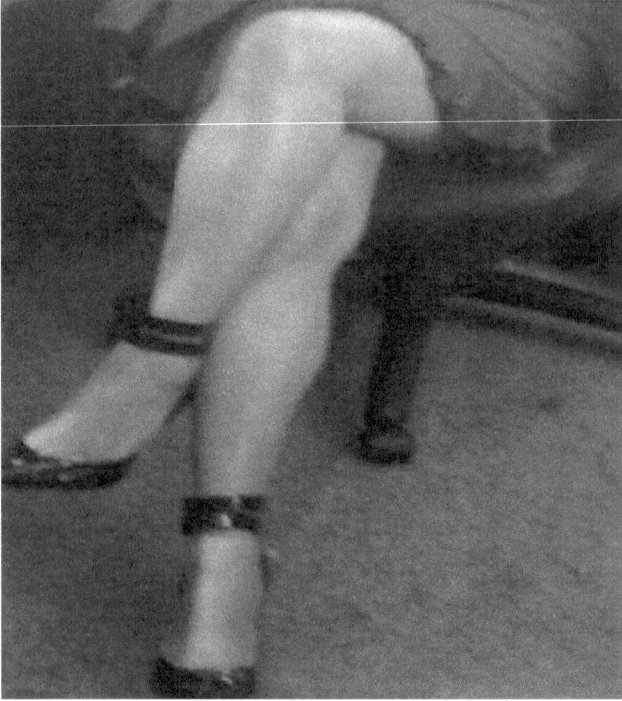

# DESIRE

There is no mystery here
Only the fact
That love and desire are not equal
Though both possess the burning, the fire, and the flame.

# FIRST IMPRESSIONS

When you walk in the room

Power and authority enter with you

Resting on your broad shoulders

The way you hold your head

Chin high

Perfectly squared jawline

That look of presence

In your eyes

Light emitting from the depths

The wide smile you give to me

Almost childlike

And regal at the same time

How you walk with your shoulders back

Body forward

Gliding

Like you rule the earth beneath your feet

Like a king

I inhale your scent as you come closer to me

Those dark eyes in that handsome face

Making me weak and giddy

I find myself drowning

My heartbeat quickening as you pull me close

Melding with you in your embrace

Our bodies become one

And I am

Undone.

# MIRROR MIRROR

From the moment I met you

I felt you

My heart beat in your chest

And yours in mine

Separate

But intertwined

From the moment I met you

I knew you

Familiar

Like home

Laughed and cried knowing

You would understand

Hoped you would at least

Be my friend

From the moment I met you

The connection was real

You made me feel seen and heard

Through the cadence of your words.

I wasn't ready for the roller coaster ride

Je tai 'me, I love you

Meant more in my mind

Than souls thoracically connected

Outside of time.

My heart beats in your chest
And yours in mine.

Diametrically opposed
We bridged the gap
Between your soul and mine
Like foes united
Through space and time
Somehow
My heart beats in your chest
My heart beats in your chest
My heart beats in your chest
          And yours in mine.

# SOUL MATES

I wanted to lie naked with you

>And silent

>Side by side

>Our hands barely touching

>Fingertips intertwined

>Bone of my bone

>And flesh

>Meeting thighs.

I wanted to lie naked with you

>In silence

>Nothing but our hearts speaking

>In a language only we know

>You and I

>Solitary

>Where I end, you begin

>Where you end, there am I.

I wanted to lie naked with you

>Through silence

>Listening to the thunder and rain

>Clapping its hands around us

>Understanding

>How much we've collectively endured and still

>We remain lovers and friends

>Alone, apart, together

>And silent.

# DEARLY BELOVED

I cannot sleep

Haunted by the rare longing of your lips on mine

Dreaming of being held firmly in your arms

Out of the blue

I miss the timber of your voice

Even though we have not spoken in a long time

Miss

How your eyes light up with joy and laughter

Or look pensive and thoughtful when we meet

I wonder if all is well with you.

If truly, as you say, there is a time for us

In this life

Or the next

We are so far apart

And yet you are still

So dearly loved.

# EXPOSED

I love him deeply,

Not a secret no one knows about for sure

I am

Naked

For all the world to see

Spoken for

Uncovered

Vulnerable

Yet

For some unknown, inexplicable reason

I am ashamed

And afraid.

No longer hiding in love

I am standing

Out in the open

And I am afraid

And ashamed.

Afraid to speak about a love I almost rejected

Afraid to own the love that he gives

In case it is false

In case it is untrue

Afraid to boast about

Being in love again.

I am naked

In front of people I don't know

Who don't know me

But will judge me

By what he says

And what they think they see

How I walk

And talk

And act

And appear

Afraid

They still will not see me

Even though I am naked

And exposed.


I stand here in my own light

Filtering myself

Afraid to boast about something that might end

Abruptly

Without warning because

Relationships can be such fragile things

And I've been cut by broken glass

And broken promises

 Before.

I'm still wearing the scars

Visible

Yet I stand here

Exposed

Naked

Though I will not cover myself

Nor will I allow myself to be ignored

So I stand behind the glow that is my own

Acknowledging my fear

And having the courage

To be fully present.

# RAW

You loved me down to my soul

>From stroking my tangled hair

>To massaging my tender toes

>Caressed my busy mind

>With laughter and ease

>Stroked the fires of inner passions and creativity

You loved me down to my soul

>Loved me way down deep

>Where none but you

>Were brave enough to go

>Never knew love like this

>Could exist

>Raw bliss

>Our love creating magic

>Spirit tripping

>We laughed and cried inside out tears

>Extravagant joy

>Exuberant, crazy, sad, and lazy

You loved me down to my soul

>In those early morning hours

>Before the birds began singing

>Before dark became daylight

>I rode you like morning dew on treetops

>And watched your eyes

>Love me down to my soul

You loved me down to my soul

       With thunder in your heartbeat

       Loved me beyond normal reach

       Down my spine

       Through my fingertips

       Your heart to my heart

       With words

       And wisdom

       And knowing

       We have been here before

       You and I

       Before the earth began

You loved me down to my soul

       To the nucleus of my being

       Performing an angioplasty on the broken and clogged

       Aortas in my life

       Scalpel, suture, healing, recovery

       You were there

       Giving sight to my organs

       That see better than my eyes

You loved me imperfectly

Raw, real, uncensored

You loved me

Down to my soul.

# RIVERS

I love you like a river

At sunrise

Quiet

Calm

The light of day glistening off its edges

Turning brown basins sea water blue

The light of the sun dancing

Skipping

Playing across the glassy endless water.


I love you like a river

When it storms

Its banks swollen with rage

Violent and cresting

Rushing the shore

Spilling over and into

Roads and houses

Making quicksand out of dry land.


I love you like a river

A tsunami

Destructive in its power

Thrusting itself vigorously, relentlessly upon the shore

A reign of horrible, sensually moaning waves.

I love you like a river

In the cool of the evening

Or at early morn

Lazy

Peaceful

Playful

Free.

# MATRIMONY

Before this

I lived life in a series of deep breaths

Short gasps

Redundant metered rhythms

I admit

I never really paid attention

To everyday moments

Until I lay for long minutes

Where my hands hurt

And I couldn't curl them to hold your hand

Or grab your hair.

The bands around my ankles now

Like slave chains

Invisible steel cuffs linked and tightened

Distinctly different from your hands

Wrapped around my ankles

Pulling me in slow motion toward you

Resting them on your shoulders

Now

There is only the numbness

And stinging like hot razor blades

From the top of my thighs

To the edge of my toenails

That can only be relieved

By the roughness of your hands

That invokes the pain

Before the pressure and pleasure comes

As you hold my legs

In your vice grip.

I cannot come to you as before

Sliding on soft sheets

Toward the ecstasy that I'm sure awaits me

I wait now instead

For the pain to ease

Pain and numbness that shuts down my womb

Deadness

You thrust deep and long to resurrect me

But I can't feel

Anything

Though your dam breaks

In the internal flood of mine

Bursting

Convulsing

Shattering

Hot waves cascading like lava

I find pleasure in your groans alone

I watch you sleep

Exhausted from the effort

Of pleasing me.

I sleep and wake up once again

To the pain

And the raging fire

And all the moments before

Disappear

Moments in a series of deep meaningful breaths

Short gasps

And resplendent metered rhythms.


I never paid attention to the everyday moments

The stabbing pains between my shoulder blades

Once strong and able to carry weight

Betray me

My entire body

A prisoner

Locked in an unwanted embrace

Solitary confinement

A shroud

A living tomb

You try to ease the tension in my still muscular calves

Your face intense

Holding back tears

For the woman you once knew

And still love

Whose legs you held so many times

On your lap

On your shoulders

Trembling

With the weight and bliss of love

And sexual satisfaction

Once upon a time

Screaming

Life

Eyes wide open

We gazed upon one another

Living

Together

In a series of deep breaths

Short gasps

Studied metered rhythms

We both pay attention

Now.

# KRYPTONITE

Lois Lane

Was Superman's kryptonite

The love he received

The love he gave

The love he craved

The love that made him weak

Even when his heart would leap buildings

In a single bound

To save her

The love that made him strong

Also made him weak

Willing to give up all his power

He loved her so

He made her forget everything they had known

All that had gone before

So she would not feel the pain

Of unrequited love

He erased the memory of him

Of them

Together

And became super again

But no one

Could erase the memory of her

From him.

He loved her so

He died to himself

He died for her

In exchange

For saving the world.

# BREATHLESS

I am in love

Still in love with a man who stole my breath away

Still can't stop not breathing

Even though his love imploded my insides

Shattered me till there was only a black

Gaping

Wound

Acrimonious hole

Ashes to ashes

And dust

He shattered my soul

Still

I am in love with the man

Who took my last breath

They said another man would come along

To fill the void

Make me forget the wounds

That refused to heal

But I remember

Most times

I only forget for a little while

A moment

While I'm getting my shoulders massaged

Or a sexual itch scratched

Then a scent

A sound

A whisper

A word

And, time traveling

There he is again


He said he was proud

My new friend and paramour

His replacement

I'm proud of you, he said

When I shredded all the pictures

Burned the letters

Packed his stuff in boxes for goodwill

Disposed of the memories

Did not call

Or write

Or inquire about him anymore

He was proud

Said I was strong

Guess he never learned that rivers

Floods

Or blazing fire

Can quench the connection

Break its hold

I smile


So he does not see the oxygen mask

He does not know

That I am still not breathing

Breathlessly, insanely in love

With the man who stole my soul

My friends are right

He is cruel to remind me at his convenience

Of what we had

What we were to each other

To keep me tethered to him

While he roams aimlessly

From one woman to another

Telling me what we could have been

If only

Leaving me

Constantly

Breathless.

# DISTRACTED

I am daydreaming again

Dreaming of wrapped in your arms

Smiling

Laughing

Cracking jokes

Tussling

I am daydreaming about you

Making love to me

Touching me with warm hands

Smothering me with kisses

Licking me in places that make my back arch

My hips rotating in delighted waves

You beside me

Inside of me

I am distracted

Daydreaming

I yearn for you

The smell of your cologne

The way your presence dominates a room

Your slow easy smile or the little boy grin

The voracious love you make

Taking me into your storm

I long for you

The passion like liquid gold in your brown eyes

Calling to me

Weakening my resolve every single time

I long for you

Your long muscular legs, flat belly, and corded arms

The hollow of your thigh

The erection tap tapping me for attention

Speaking to me

Calling me to come

Cum

I long for you

Like light to the day and stars to the night

My body calls to you

Come to me

Cum through me

I long for you

Distraction.

# DESIRE

I want you

Want you like water to a thirsty man

Like life to the dying

Like the spirit that needs a body to dwell in

I need you

Need you like flowers need rain

Like a starving man needs sustenance

Like air and oxygen

This doesn't make sense

We just met

Imagining things

Holding onto myself

Afraid of falling

Euphoria

Transfixed

Mesmerized

Desire

# RAIN

Makin' love with you

Is like playing in the rain on a sunny day

Like water in the desert

Like ice cream soda

Or seeing the acrobats at the circus for the first time

Like hot chocolate

And thunder showers with no umbrella

Like fire

Or drowning in a solitary puddle

Making love to you

With you

Is like playing in the rain.

# ALPHA AND OMEGA

You were my crush

The one I didn't have in high school

Or college

Or any place in between

You know

The ones your girlfriends talk about in the locker room at school

Or sitting at a table drinking soda

At a Black student union affair

You were the before and after

The beginning and the end

The alpha and omega

I was so in love with you

No one else would do.

# CRUSH

I wish I could tell you

    How your smile brightens my day

    Because you smile with your eyes

    And your entire face lights up

    Unforced and genuine

I hear your compliments and ignore them

Thinking

I know he says that to all the girls

Like a 30-minute delay

They hit me later

I think about what you said and wonder.

# VALENTINE

Connection can neither be created nor destroyed

Like atoms and molecules

Ever present

At least that's what they said in science class

And sociology

But who can tell me how you and I connected so effortlessly?

On that first night

Your body fused naturally to mine as we danced

Our conversation, like two old friends meeting

Though we'd never engaged before.


Connection can neither be created nor destroyed

So why, to this very day, no matter how many miles apart

Or years that separate us

In my heart

You're never far away


You're my secret secret

I keep hidden from all eyes

You're my favorite secret

My undercover surprise.

You don't even know it

That I always see forever in your eyes.

Connection can neither be created nor destroyed

At least that's what they tell me

So does this mean

Scientifically

That I was always in your heart

And you in mine

Valentine

# NO REGRETS

I will never regret having loved and lost

       Loved greatly and fully with expectancy

       Loved foolishly and with undue admiration

       Loved dangerously, passionately, and frivolously

No

I will never regret having loved with all that is within me

# CHAPTER THREE

# SWORDS AND SHIELDS

We run for cover
From things we don't understand
To shield ourselves
From pressure
Pain
And death.

# MASTERPIECE

I was your masterpiece

Or so I think you think

It's in the way you look at me

All proud and distant

Admiring the work of my hands

As though it were yours

You sit me on your mantle to admire and claim

Mine

# MIRANDA

You have the right to remain silent

But I'm asking you to talk to me

To tell me what is on your mind.

You have the right to remain silent

But I asked you to tell me what you want

What do you need from me

You gave silence, nothing, air and space

What am I supposed to do with that

I am not clairvoyant, not trying to predict the future

Or read your mind

But I understand

You have the right

To remain

Silent

And alone.

# CRAVINGS AND LEFTOVERS

I craved you

Like hot wax on candles

Dark chocolate and strawberries

Moonlight and music

And all my favorite things

I can still hear you

Singing in my ear

Whispering to me as we made love

I thought of you

Every moment of every day

Daydreaming about what we shared

You were my king

And I cried out for your presence

The presence you've taken from me

The throne of my heart sagged from the weight

Of waiting

Of missing

You were

Cravings and leftovers.

# DO THE MATH

I am a multiplier

I multiply wisdom, attention, love, affection and energy

Whatever you give to me

I give it back exponentially

Negative zero

I can multiply that too

And give you less

You build me up

I multiply that and upgrade you

You tear me down

I multiply that

And destroy you too

I am a multiplier

So be careful what you give to me

Be careful what seeds you sow

Because I will incubate

And multiply one hundred

One thousand

Ten thousand-fold

Before you give me lame excuses

And your pocket full of lies

Remember, I am a mathematician

And I multiply.

# SWORDS AND SHIELDS

We came at each other like combatants on a battlefield

Two swords

Two shields

We cut each other

Bleeding

Held up our shields

In a defensive stance

Not recognizing that the battle was long over

The victories already won

And done

We came at each other like two combatants on a battlefield

Where love was supposed to reign supreme

But

We had been at war in the world so long

With ourselves

And others

We didn't know

Didn't recognize

That it was time

To lay down our weapons

To discard our defenses

And just be

So

Instead

We came at each other like armed soldiers

On a battlefield

Where the only enemy that existed

Was us

And we both

Lost.

# MESSY

I know I should walk away

I am not blind, deaf, or dumb

I recognize the red flags

And calling cards from spirit saying

Not now

Not yet

Maybe not ever

And it hurts


I pretend to be brave

But it hurts walking away

Staying away

From someone who I once thought

Was knit

To my soul

# DEVASTATION

I am hovering somewhere between madness

Mayhem

And monstrosity

I look at myself in the mirror

And find nothing appealing

I am most miserable today

And it is my fault

Certainly my fault

I called it off

I said, "Stop, who goes there?"

In my Hamlet and Macbeth tone.

Today I feel crossed out

Crossed over

Overlooked and unidentifiable

How long am I going to stare out this window

Hoping that I see him roll up

You crazy bastard

You told him you were afraid

You told him from the beginning you were skittish

Asked him to please be careful with you

You said you were a runner

Hi didn't care

Challenge accepted.

Today I am the monstrosity

The monster under the bed

Hovering between what you said

And what you did and did not do

Not understanding the why of me and you.

Marry me

You asked me out of the blue

Then pushed me away

Too soon

I barely know you

Though I see the you that you present

Who are you?


Today I am a monster

A disheveled ugly thing

Head in my hands

Sinuses blocked

Chest tight from tears I can't cry

So many tears

A river

A lake

An ocean

How did you make me cry so many tears

And we've only just met.

Today I am disfigured in my grief

Hating myself

Familiar animal

I've been here before

Monstrosity

A mess

Devastated

Confused

Questioning

You really tried to make me hate me

Now I'm trying

Not to hate you.

# PRETENDER

I wanted to love you with my whole heart

Not give you parts of me

But you were so busy pretending

Putting on a show for everyone else

Trying to look like a superhero

I see that you are a star

I know your potential

Your inherent gifts, skills, talents, abilities

I see you

Stepping down from your throne

To walk

And live

And act

Like a common man

I see who you really are

Even when you set aside your crown

I accept you as is

But you are so busy pretending

Putting on a show for everyone else

Trying to look like a superhero

Blinded by the light of adoration

You play-acted

Taking for granted the love right in front of your face


You didn't need to perform for me

But you loved the audience

Had to have the cheers from the crowd

So I took my heart

And made my exit

Stage left.

# ROLL UP

Why you roll up in my life

If you wasn't ready

On some other shit

I ain't got time for this

Playing Mr. Invisible

Cause you fucked up what was important to me

You in hiding

Can't pick up a phone to call and talk to me

Bitch, we ain't kids

Too grown for this motherfucking shit

Stay gone

Yeah, I know I'll miss your presence and your smile

But I'll get over it

Why you roll up in my life though?

What did you really see

When you saw me?

What did you really want?

What did you really need?

For the first time

Be honest

I was a mark

But you didn't know

Where I'd already gone in my life.

Can't gaslight and manipulate me

Into living and breathing

Your reality

Brother, I've been with the master of the game

And I learned well

So, these games you play

Are kids-play

You marked me

Thought I was weak and frail

Saw my disability

You marked me

Rolled up in my life cause you thought I was easy

Poured on the charm, the charisma, good sex, and spirituality

But you got caught in the crossfire

Of your own vanity

I have to thank you though

Cause you ushered me back to my spiritual roots

Set me on this new path

And helped me to remember

The value of my own voice.

# TOO CLOSE

You know me

But you don't respect what you know

And that

Is your

Undoing


Why you mad

I don't return your phone calls

After you done put me on the back burner for days?

Is that the game we playin'?

Why you upset

When we set a date and time

That you don't prepare for

And I say never mind?

Which chick you think you was wit this time?


You know me

But you don't respect what you know

And that

Is your undoing.


What's that face about?

That puppy dog pout

Knowing I no longer give a damn

Cause you done did more talking

Then walking the walk

You talk about

Got me lookin' at you like I can't trust you

You taught me not to

Coming back and forth

With the same words

The same lies

Cover up, manipulate, gaslight yourself

On fire

And you mad for burning up you?

You play the same hand

Ain't nothin' new

I've played that hand too

Your switch up game done got crossed over

Cause I know you

And you know me too

But you still looking for the keys to the vault

Where all my treasures lie

Been tryna figure out the combination for a long, long time

Cause you figure you know me

And on a lot of levels you do

But you don't respect what you know

And that is your undoing.

# OFFENDED

Soft

Soft as a newborn baby's behind

And tender

That's how you are

Soft

With no spine erected

Newborn

Stillborn

Soft

Allowing words you receive

Through warped and wounded perception

To change

And channel your whole life

Into pitiful whiny baby soft

Cries

Whining

You are

Always

Whining

So soft

Kid glove soft

Asshole soft

Tissue paper soft

Soft piles of fallen leaves

Wildly flying in the wind

Cracking under the crush of feet

Like dust

You float away

To nothing

Useless

Dried

Soft

Dust

# NOTHIN' BUT A SANDWICH

Patience is not what I do well

I want

What I want

When and how I want it

So I'm asking myself

Self

Are you ready to walk away

Cause patience is not in my vocabulary today

I want what I want

When and how I want it

If I must wait too long

I'm gone.


I value time

And you ain't wasting mine

Ain't wasting what I can't get back

For what

A snack

No sir

You ain't nothing but a sandwich

And I haven't got the patience to stand in line

For a happy meal.

# NINE LIVES

He loved me

And I loved him too

Yet that was not enough

When times got tough

It was too much


He loved me

Said he did

I said it too

We loved

Maybe

Till the baby came

And he got strange


He loved me

Said he loved me

And I loved him too

Too much it seems

I know

It's true

But what was I to do

I loved him so

But I had to go

He would have loved me to death

My own

He loved me

And I loved him too

But he wanted worship

And that wouldn't do

So I left him too


You say you're in love with me

And I wonder

What does that mean

I don't know

I guess I love you too

And you love me?

We'll see.

# TAPPED OUT

I poured into you

And you drank

Thirsty

I fed you from a plate of peace

And you ate

Greedy

You offered your lust

Rage

And negativity

Malnourished

I capped the fountain

Leaving you to feast on your own misery.

# MELODRAMA

Why are you here in my life

Again?

What did you come for this time?

What do you need now?

I let you go three times

But you come back like a damn boomerang

A bad dream

Last time

Felt sure

I would never see you again

Was satisfied

Set free

Finally

But here you are again

Turning up in my life on repeat

Trying to tune in

Talking bout you care for me

Fuck outa here!

Be real

Why are you here now?

What's gone wrong in your life this time

That you expect me to heal and make right?

# HEARTLESS

You asked for my heart

And I gave it to you

Cautious

I was

At first

But you swept me off my feet

You asked me for my heart

Poured love all over me

In me

Around me

Through me

Till I relented

And

Willingly

Gave it to you

Without reservation

Heart of my heart

Till your heart beat in mine

You asked me for my heart

And I gave it to you

And you walked away with it

Snuck off in silence

An incredible disappearing act so thorough

I can't feel my heart beating anymore

You asked me for my heart

And you stole it

Took it away with you

Not a whisper

Not a word

Not a sound.

# THE ONE

I keep thinking

This is the one

This is the one that will make me forget

What it means to be one

This

Is the one who will erase your name

Your face from my memory

I keep hoping

This is the one

Who will love me just as I am

But I have discovered

That am the one

I've been searching for.

# CHAPTER FOUR

# SAVIOURS AND SERPENTS

We are our own worst enemy
The one in the mirror reflects
Hides
Or denies
The true character of the image
We can't see inside.

# I AM NOT YOUR SAVIOUR

I understand you

But I wasn't sent to your life to redeem you

I am not the rescue squad


I see you

But I wasn't sent to your life

To give you vision

I wasn't gifted with giving sight

To the blind


I acknowledge your pain

But I am not your healer

      The doctor

      Or the physician

I am here

Because you called me

I came

Because you requested my presence

But I am not here

To make it all better for you

At the expense of me

I am not your savior

You must come to your own healing

For yourself.

# SERPENTS

It wasn't him that I left

I shook off the poisonous serpents

That were inside of him

That tried to attach themselves to me.

Snakeskin shoes look mighty fine

But the snake who wears them

Is still a reptile

Full of venomous love

And girl you so fine

Serving salacious sex

With an insidious smile

Inserting streams of venom

To take your life for a while

Within the poison

There is the cure

Girl, do you know

That you are the antidote

Chop that snake's head off

Render his liquid powerless

Crush it under your feet

And get on about your business.

# CHOOSE AGAIN

I settled for you

But I can choose again

I settled for crumbs from your table of time and emotion

I settled for morsels of attention and affection

I settled for you

But I can choose again

I settled for company as a substitute for partnership

I settled for words with no immediate action

If there was any action taken at all

I settled for dreaming without direction

I settled for you

And it took me some time to be aware

Not as long as it used to

That I had settled for you

I walked away

Recognizing that I do have the option

To choose again.

# FROM WHAT I'M TOLD

From what I'm told

You never forget a good woman

You never lose the memory

    Of the mornings she cooked breakfast for you

    Massaged warm oil into your back,

        And shoulders

        And hips

        And thighs

    Cause you were hurting.

You will never forget how she

    Stroked your head

    Both of them

    When your mind was too full

    Of the weight men carry

    How she

    Held your hand

    And eased your soul

    As shock waves coursed through your body

You will never forget

    Her sweet voice

    Encouraging you to breathe

    Slow

    Breathe

Deep

       When pain shot through you

       And words wouldn't come

You will never forget

       How she listened to your dreams

       And stories

       How she cried and laughed with you

       The days she took your hands in hers

       And prayed for you.

From what I'm told

       You will never erase

       The mark of a good woman

       And though you try to replace her

       And maybe you'll succeed

       You will never forget what it felt like

       To be loved beyond your need.

# MY MOST UNLOVELY SELF

I stood by my most unlovely self

And held my arms out to me

When the world changed

And I became different.


I no longer cared about showing up lovely

Or being admired

I didn't care about getting things done decently

And in order

I abandoned the waste of perfection

Didn't care about the dimples and stretch marks

At the back of my thighs

Or how my stomach pokes out

Leading me around

The hair on my head no longer shiny

With its golden brown and reddish hues

I am

Satisfied to be plain

The freckles dotting my face, my back now, and my arms

I dare to connect the dots

To understand myself


I don't care that my bad eyesight

And keen insight

Mirrors my rotten attitude

You look like nothing from a distance

And up close

A blob

An inanimate creature

A thing that I'm not interested in knowing

I beg you to keep your distance

So I won't have to cut you down to size

With this dagger on my tongue.


My nail polish is chipped

I don't have a Colgate smile

I don't care for smiling now

Keep your epithets to yourself

       "it's gonna get better'

       "keep your head up'

       'God got you"

I don't want to hear none of that

All those things you say to make you feel better

Leaves me feeling like punching you in the mouth.


I stand by my most unlovely self

And make love to me

Naked

Unashamed

I think of no one else

As I please myself

I stand by my most imperfect self

Unconcerned about your should not

    What if

    And if only

Opinion ass cracks

We all have 'em

Everybody's shit stinks

Why are you so concerned with sniffing mine?

I have acknowledged my weaknesses

Applauded the strengths that I birthed out of struggle

    And trauma

    Pain

    And death

I stand by my most unlovely wounded self

Every day

I come into the world disrobed and distorted

Giving birth to me

Again.

# ESCAPE HATCH

I find myself trying

Always

To escape

Frequently

I run into these words

To escape my reality

To tell my truth

To lift myself

Or cry and scream and holler and sigh

To escape my dreams

And the nightmares that come

When my mind refuses to sleep well

And it's dark in the house

Feeling the need to analyze all the stuff

In my head

When sleep offers no remedy

I write

Running into words

That set me free.

# SCORPION

Sometimes I be trippin'

Doing petty shit

Just to get under people's skin

Especially people who annoy me

I love making my haters hate me more

Gives me a particular thrill

I set traps

And watch them fall in

Then laugh

Cause I'm vindictive

And petty

Like a scorpion

I measure my sting

And strike

Unexpected

I know how lethal I am

I can give just enough to bruise the heel

Watch you writhe in pain

Knowing that within my venom

Is also the antidote

In me is the cure

But there are those

Who hate cures

Preferring the curse

Laughing

I let them have it all

Again and again

Repetitively

Cause I'm petty

And I like to watch your stupid ass

Squirm

# PREVARICATION

Lie to me again

Tell me one more time

How much you love me

How lovesick you are each minute you spend

Away from me

Lie to me again

Play with my head

One more time

Pierce my heart with schemes and deception

Lie to me again and pretend

That you love me

That you love anyone

Lie to my face one more time

Silence

Cold neckline

Blood on my sleeve

You can't breathe?

Words won't come?

I know

It's over

# DREAM GIRL

You are every man's dream

That's what he said

Dreamed of having a woman like me

But it seems

The dreamer

Has a tough time dealing with reality

To him

I was merely a dream

A fantasy

An illusion

In reality

He made me invisible

Vanquished to enigmatic silhouettes

A mystic foggy haze

But I am real

With feelings, desires, emotions, needs

And dreams of my own

Since, in his mind,

I was an illusion

I insisted that he forget my name

Forget I ever existed in his reality

As I am just

Something he dreamed up.

# BANKRUPT

I have loved and lost

So many times

I have been bankrupted

My soul battered

My spirit weak

My heartbeat faint

I have been broken so many times in love

I wonder if I know what love is at all

I wonder, as much as you love me

  As much as you say you do

  Will you leave me broken and fragile too

I put on my running shoes just in case

I have to get ready, set, go

Away from you

Distrustful, fearful, anxious

Is the joy I feel when I'm with you an illusion

How you hold my hand and watch

For all the monsters you may have to fight

To protect me

How territorial you are

How you love me with your heart visible in your eyes

I want to be with you

Even though I'm afraid to ask for forever

Cause I have been bankrupted by love

My "specialness" not special enough

Beauty you say you behold

Not enough

> Kindness, sweetness, intelligence, compassion

> "I love talking to you"

> "You always make me feel better"

> "Damn, you're sexy."

> "I wish I had met you when…"

Not enough

No matter what they said

I have been constantly relegated to that *special place*

That little four by four thought somewhere in his chest

When what I wanted was a heart

To love me

I don't give a damn about those special places

I'd rather you forget that I exist

Then relegate me to a corner of your mind

To think about in your spare time

Man, she was a good wife

> My best friend

> The best lover I ever had

Bullshit

I've heard it all

I'd rather you forget me

Then remember me in that special place

While you hold someone else in your arms.

# THE LAST LETTER

I tried to write to you

Put into words all the things I've felt

Things I wanted to say and didn't

Things I wanted to do

But I couldn't bring myself to finish

I tried to write you a letter

But I couldn't find the words to say

      I'm breaking

      Dismantling myself bit by bit

Couldn't find the words because

I'm trying not to be broken again.


I tried to write to you

Yesterday

And the day before

And every day I've said goodbye

And hello again

I cried

Tearless

Heartless

Empty

And I was ok with that

But I couldn't write you and tell you that

It would have hurt your feelings

And I know

Despite how tough you imagine yourself to be

How very fragile you really are.

I tried to write to you

To tell you about the numbness

The wearing away

The faded smiles

And thinly veiled fear

That fear you know so well

The fear of losing everything

Including yourself

I tried to write to you but

The words wouldn't come

How do you emphatically and unequivocally say

Enough and

Grow up.

# EPILOGUE

Yesterday

I dreamed you

Daydreamed

Night dreamed

Nightmares

Fantasies

You and me

Living in a great big house in South Carolina

Calling to our grandchildren from the porch

As they play in the yard and

Chasing each other around our wrap-around porch

A house we built with our own hands

I tried to write you a letter

But I couldn't explain the dream

Or believe in it.

Tried to get all the words down just right

But all my thoughts, and dreams

Fantasies and realties

Notions and not-so

Merged

And I could not write to you at all

So, I wrote this poem instead.

# CHAPTER FIVE

# INTO THE ROOM

Last rites
Last words
What else is there to say

# FIRSTBORN

Robert Alan Powell II

That was the government name

Of my first-born son.

Named after his father

And looked just like his senior

From day one.

My husband and I

Were both proud and fascinated with our baby's

Tiny square tipped ears

Perfectly round cheeks

And straight black cap of hair fastened to a large round head

That had ripped me from stem to stern.

I played with his tiny hands

While his dad counted fingers and toes.

How incredulous we were that we could bring a whole new life

Kicking and screaming

Into the world

Born four days before my 23rd birthday,

He was sickly

And greedy, nursing every hour on the hour

He grew strong

     Intense

     Intelligent

     Compassionate

     Competitive

     Funny and stoic at the same time

He intimidated strangers

But he was a tender touch to those he knew and loved

He grew to manhood

Six foot two, athletic and muscular

With a face for photography

And the arrogance borne of good looks, intelligence, and confidence

 He was loved and admired by many

Too many

His love of family was his hallmark

And he was the loving, protective thread that kept us all together.

Then the dreams came.

The dreams that neither of us recognized as premonitions

The dreams that turned into real life nightmares.

He dreamed he was fighting three people.

I dreamed of a young man

His height and build

Laying in a pool of blood around his head.

A man whose face I could not see

Two days later

A mere two days after we both dreamed

A hospital surgeon was telling me

My son

My firstborn

My beautiful baby boy

Would not live more than two hours

Maybe four

They named him Lenny Trauma

The last words he had said

As he swung me around and kissed my face

Were

I love you

The last words I said

Laughing and punching his arm as he put me down

Were

I love you

The last words we said to one another

Were

Muddah

Son

I love you

I never heard his voice again.


My baby, my firstborn

Was 29 years old when he passed

Three years older than my father had been

Twenty-nine years older than his firstborn son

I felt him leave me

Even before his last breath

When no one really knew he was going

I felt him leaving me

His spirit and mine so intertwined


Bobby and I had plans

He had dreams

Just like my baby brother

Who I lost too

We talked often about dreams

So many dreams

But on a bright October day

Heaven came

And took my firstborn son away

Suddenly

And forever

I will never be the same

I cry when I see his face

Or hear his name

One year

Five years

Ten

It all feels the same

Heaven came

And took my firstborn son away.

# MUDDAH

Do you know

That every time I see your picture

I want to pull you off the page

And hold you in my arms again

Like when you were a little boy

Do you know

Do you even know my name

I am your mother


Do you know

That I say that every time I see you

Hope you look at me just one time

Just one time

Like you recognize me

Like you remember

And I never know if you do or not

I hope and I pray

But I don't know

Cause you don't

Can't

Squeeze my hand to tell me so


Do you know

Last night I watched an old video

Hoping to get glimpses of you in motion

Smiling, laughing, dancing, waving, anything

Yearning to see you moving

Not still

And broken like you are now

I longed to see you

Alive and well again


Do you know

I keep your baby picture in my room now

I don't hang it up anymore

Because it reminds me

I can't pick you up

And make it all better now

But I still sing to you

Do you know that

I still sing to you

The same song

God bless the child

Do you remember how you used to fall asleep

Every time

Even when you were a teenager

So, I sing to you

Even though you're a grown man.


Do you know how very much I love you.

Do you know how very much I miss you.

Do you even remember my name.

I'm your "Muddah"

# INTO THE ROOM ·

I thought the pain would go away

That it would not hurt so much

As it did yesterday

But yesterday and today are twins

Alike in every way

The pain never ends

Not mine. Not yours. Not theirs.

It nudges me awake every morning

And lays down beside me

     On top of me

     Hovering over me

     Hanging around inside of me

       Every night

       Holding my mind and memory hostage

I cannot move or think without this excruciating torturous affliction

It follows me to the train station

The bus stops

Into your room

Where I watch you

Asleep or awake

I try to put a smile on my face

Cause I don't want you to see

That pain that haunts me.

It's always there

The ghosts of it

When I hold your hand

And you struggle to reciprocate

When I stroke your face

And wonder if you even remember who I am

It's always there

Lingering

And I am so angry

I run into the hall

So you don't see me crying out to God

Screaming in silence

The tomes ringing in my head

"I want my son back! I want my son back!"

And God says no

Not yet

Not today

I am angry that I have to talk to God this way.


I thought the pain would eventually go away

But today is another day

And it still takes up residence

Here

In unholy matrimony

An alliance I didn't ask for

It refuses to go

    To leave him alone

    Or me

                Or the others

Pain, pain, torment go away

It answers

No

Not today

Not today.

# LABOR PAINS

I am giving birth again

To a six-foot tall man who was already

My first born

Who grew to be my ace

My friend

I look at his face and can see me

Even though he can't see

Me

I am giving birth

Wailing, singing, dancing, screaming

Crying in the spirit

And in the natural

Un-naturally

So that he may be born again

From my spirit womb

I am

Giving birth again

The labor pains are fierce

I've never screamed or cried giving birth before

But this time

This time I scream and sometimes

I cry all night long till I fall asleep

Wake up again

Crying

Screaming

I want my son back!

Praying

In sleep

And awake

And sometimes

I sing

And the pain subsides

I walk and feel the fresh sunshine on my face

And I am grateful for the walking

Until I remember that he can't walk

Yet

Then I walk for him more than me

Because I can

And he can't

I am

Giving birth again

To books, business, dreams

All the time wondering

What his new life will be like


Tomorrow

I go to receive an award that I had forgotten about

They are honoring me

"Women's Opportunity"

I am blessed

And in pain

Giving birth

To this new life

This new horrendously painful

Unexpected thing.

# LIFE UNTO LIFE

This morning I remember holding my newborn baby on my bare breasts

My newly male man

Blood and creamy white chunks

Still covering his naked body

His umbilical cord pulsing with life

His eyes were closed

And he screamed until we touched

Skin to skin

And I cooed over him

His calm restored

He knew this skin.

This voice.

This peace.

His father

Awed as I

Stood watching

Knowing

Amazed we had created this life together

This tiny little thing

Came from us

Life unto life

He was my baby and my world at once

He made me a mother

For the first time

And I marveled at his creation

The miracle of birth

The continuation of life unto life

A mirror of myself.

# SINS OF THE FATHERS

My son was murdered by strangers

One who knew him by name

The other who had never seen his face before

And the witness who stood in shock and never said a word

As my son

Lay dying

Unconscious

Blood welling up in his head

His brain swelling to its skull's capacity

Enough to burst

Through the shell

They watched, argued, screamed at one another

While he lay dying

Ten, twenty, thirty, ninety minutes

Before she called an ambulance

The blood filling his brain

Flowing out of his mouth

They argued

Who would take the blame

While my son

Lay dying.


My son was murdered by strangers

One who called him by his name

Yet proclaimed

She never knew him

The other

Who showed no remorse at his sentencing

After pleading guilty

And getting no real time

A stranger the prison education system applauded

"Leader" they called him

Released on "good behavior"

Eight months later

The same man who police said

Was in custody 26 times for domestic violence

His girlfriend never pressed charges

So none of it counted

Until the day

Two strangers murdered my son.


Philadelphia district attorneys

Called my son's six-foot grave

A "misdemeanor homicide"

What the hell is that?

"Mistakes were made on both sides" the judge said.

"No use destroying two lives" the judge said.

But my son is not coming back


Justice is blind

Justice never once cried.

I spent time with my son's children the other day

Two of his three daughters

I remembered

The strange ones also had a son

I pray the sins of the father

And the mother

Are not visited upon that one.

The strangers were home with their children for Christmas

My son's children visited their daddy's grave.


I don't have forgiveness to give

Only prayers for the children

Who don't deserve the bill

For the sins of the fathers.

# TICK-TOCK

I'm glad he couldn't hear the clock ticking

Didn't realize the passage of time

The year he lost when he lost himself

To un-consciousness

Semi-consciousness

And finally fully awake

With no voice

And wondering eyes

Living

But not fully alive

I am grateful for the things he did not know

The damage

The surgeries

And why

The severe TBI.


Love's predominating factor is unselfishness

That is why he stayed

Love baring pain unselfishly for so long

That is why he went away

As much as we wanted him to stay

As much as we loved him, needed him

As much as we wanted to hold onto our beloved

One more day

Love

Was letting him go in peace

When he heard

The clock

Tick-tock.

# THE INVESTIGATION

Who did you look for?

What evidence did you secure?

Why did she go free?

Why was his sentence much less than it should be?

You already know

Who dealt the final blow

You already said

Justice will come in the end

But the wheels of justice still grind slow

So slow

They've come to a screeching halt.

You and I know who was at fault

They say karma is a bitch

Well

I keep hoping

I'm around to see it

Cause justice

Is just

A glitch.

# BLURRED VISION

I used to wear rose colored glasses

And see everything through love filled eyes

Now I wear shades

And see things in black and white

The darkness

Before the light.

# RIPPED

Rip out my heart now!

Please

Rip it out of my chest with no anesthesia

So I don't feel anything

Do it quickly

Please

I'm begging


Rip out my heart

Quickly

Cleanly

Cause I swear I'm tired of feeling this pain

Please

Please

Please

Somebody rip out my damn heart!

# WHAT ELSE - A CONVERSATION WITH GOD

What else

What else will you take from me

I am not strong

I don't know why people keep saying that

What else

What else will you take from me

No one and nothing is mine

I know that now

So tell me

What else

What else will you take from me

Before I lose my mind?

# THE WORD

In the beginning was the word

And the word was made flesh and blood

In the beginning was the word

I love you

Marry me

Let's have a baby

And the word became flesh and blood

Seven pounds, fourteen ounces, twenty-one inches

Of the word made flesh

And blood

In the end was the word

And the blood

That stained the floor

Gathering in a pool around his head

As they stood above him

Arguing

And he didn't move

In the end was the word

Subdural hematoma

Global damage to the brain

 I love you

I'm going

Screaming

I want my son back

Afterwards

There were no words

Only the darkness

Empty

Void


In the end

There were no words

Only darkness

And silence

# AFTERSHOCK

I should walk now

I should walk outside and see the sky

Sunlight

Trees

Cars riding by

I should walk now

Past the coffin

And the grave clothes

Past the mourners

And the headstones

In my head

I should walk now

Go outside and see something

Besides your last breath

Your bare chest

With no heartbeat

Your skin

Pale and lifeless

Your mocha overpowered by milk skin

I should go outside now.

My heart won't let me.

Since you stopped breathing

Can't breathe since you left me.

The darkness abounds

All around

Inside and outside

Silence where your voice used to be

Can't hear you talk about dreams

Laugh when we agree.

We were born to change the world.

We were born to change

You were born to change the world.

You were born to grow

And change

Yet you are gone.


I'm tired.

So tired

Too tired to get out of this bed and open a window.

Too tired to crack the shade.

Too tired to lift the covers off my legs

Though the heat in the room is too much

I want to sleep

Forever


I should walk now.

I sit up

Awake


I write

Observe the world through cracks of shade light

Hear the outside come in knowing

I should get up

Get out of bed

Get washed, dressed

Too much

I should walk now

But I see your face

Your translucent dying face

Where the blood has gone

My hand on your heart

That has stopped beating

And I lay down again.

# RAINBOW CHILD

I am a rainbow child

My anger as black as the night sky without stars

My rage white hot

Burning holes in the atmosphere

My eyes blood red

From crying over blood shed

I am a rainbow child.


I am a rainbow child

My sadness arching a somber blue aura

Louis Armstrong blues blue

Cause I love you my son

Who was called up yonder

Way too soon

Leaving me in shades of grey grief

I am a rainbow child.


I am a rainbow child

My spirit the hue of dull brown mud

That covers your grave now

As rain

And snow

Moisten and harden the cold ground


Where you lay now

My soul is muddy brown

And I drown

Constantly

In quicker sand than I can hold my head up in

Wishing I could see and touch your brown skin

With my hands again

I am every dull and colorless hue

Without you

Bleeding the rainbow of its fluorescent streams

That symbol of hope

I remain hopeless

I live and exist in the

Bereft of light

I am a dark rainbow child.

# NOW I LAY ME DOWN TO WEEP

I drove up to the cemetery today

Don't know why it gives me so much peace

This place of the deceased

It's beautiful

So well kept

I brake for the geese that cross my path

They are here in droves

I look again for the deer on the hill

Where your body rests in peace

In front of a tree they said was evergreen

Even though I knew they lied

I was okay with it

Even now as I watch its green leaves

Turn blood red

Capturing the sunlight

That blinds me

It is so beautiful here

And so peaceful

Where you lay

Eternally

Sitting alone

And separate

On a hill

Beneath a beautiful

Scarlet tree

I lay on the ground

Next to your gravestone

And weep.

# GRAVES

I buried him ten years ago

Hard to believe

It's been such a long time

Since I watched him die

And still

I can't talk about him

Without the tears coursing down my face

Or caught in my throat

Or closing my eyes

I remember

Your birthdays

Your childhood

And watching you grow to become a man

How you loved your little girls

And grieved your little boy

How you love

And loved

And loved

Until the day you died

And loved some more

Ten years

One hundred years

A millennial will never be enough time

To bury the memory

Of all that you are

All that you were

To so many

And to me.

# DESCENDING

The dark cloud has descended again

And I am withered by it

Rendered speechless

I turn to sleep

And alcohol

To remove the sting of feeling

Of knowing

Of missing you so terribly


I try to keep a dream

And faith

In front of me

But my heart fails

And my tongue is rooted to the top of my mouth

I am unable to speak

Everything fails

In the darkness of the cloud

Descending

# CRY

I wish I could cry out all the tears I feel

And drop them into a puddle

But they would make a lake

Then a river

Then a deep blue sea

Then an ocean

So many tears are inside of me.


I wish I could un-sing all the songs I have ever sung

Every love song

And faith song

And strength song

Because right now

At this moment

My music is gone

I have not one note to give

And what I have left

Is a cacophony of sound

All mixed up and unidentifiable

Horrible chords

And monotones

Yet

I want to hold on and protect this horrible music for a while

In case death comes for that too.

I wish I could scream

Loud

And long

And socially unacceptable screams

Scream so loud and silent only dogs, birds, bees could hear

And be sobered

And silenced

This way

My pain will not disturb the comings and goings of humanity

Because I have discovered that

No matter how I feel

Life goes on.

People go about their irresolute missions to be somewhere

Anywhere

Fast

I wish I could scream so silently loud they wouldn't feel uncomfortable.


I wish I could say all the things I left unsaid

Undo all the things I shoulda, woulda, coulda done

Sharing dreams together again

Listen more to yours and hear you better

I wish I could say all the things I wanted to say

Before pride, fear, and death got in the way.

# EPITAPH

I could have been a better sister, mother, friend

I could have done more, been more for them

I wish I could have beat back the monsters

And killed all the demons

That came and ruined their lives

Stealing them away from me

I wish I could un-cry all their tears and un-hurt all their pain

I wish I could hit something so hard it would shatter

Blink

Turn around three times

Click my heels

And bring my father

My son

My brother all back again.

# THE EDGE

I walked to the edge

And fell off

Threw myself over

Believing I could fly

Broke my back

And my legs

Screaming

Then

I stood up

And walked out of myself

Knowing

I am more than the shattered pieces

That remain.

# I HOPE FOR HEAVEN

My grandson asked me if I believed in heaven

I told him

I hope for heaven

I hope there is truly a place where my loved ones can rest in peace

And the lion can lay down with the lamb

Without tearing him to pieces

Where the ancestral spirits rest in power

Where life is not over

But eternal

I hope for heaven

Where agony and death are defeated

Swallowed up in the grave that was designed to hold them hostage

I hope for heaven

Where battles are not fought over money and power

Where children can be free to love and be loved

Instead of being preyed upon

Where the still small voice

Speaks clearly

I hope for heaven

Where light and love abound

And time is no longer fleeting.

I hope for heaven

Where there will be no more need for knights in shining armor

Or damsels in distress

No need for war or rumors thereof

I hope for heaven son

Where peace and joy abound

I sincerely hope

And pray

For heaven

# INTO THE RUINS

Come with me

And I'll show you who I am

And what this life has made me

Cut open my thoracic cavity

Reach in

Pull out my heart

Hold it beating in your hand

Blood gushing through your fingers

> Every drop a memory
>
> Of the moment
>
> The milliseconds
>
> The many times it was pierced
>
> By friends
>
> Lovers
>
> Strangers
>
> Family
>
> Loss
>
> And people claiming to give a damn

Come with me

> Damn it!

Come

Bring your cowardly ass to my realm

Walk with me through the years of disillusionment

Years where I was invisible

Battered

Abused

Neglected

Terrified

Scarred

And disfigured

I dare you to come with me

And walk among the ruins.

# CHAPTER SIX

# GHOSTS AND LAST RITES

Ghosts
Apparitions
Last rites and rituals
As the proverb says,
Every shut eye
Ain't sleep
And every goodbye
Ain't gone

# AFTERBIRTH

A man

One born with a penis

Who redefined himself

Because he could

Because he was empowered to do so

Is trying to tell me

That I am not a woman

That my menstrual I got when I was thirteen means nothing

The horrendous cramping and heavy flow

The embarrassing moments

When I overflowed onto my pristine white dress at church

Or when blood seeped through the mattress-like heavy flow pad

I wore to school one day

Spreading its crimson fingers all over the back of my light blue bell bottoms

They were my favorite pants

I threw them away.

The regular trips to the hospital

Because the cysts that continually developed on my ovaries

Made the pain so unbearable that

I frequently passed out

None of that means anything

Though having these excruciatingly painful,

Embarrassing

Horrendous periods

Result, for many of us, in the ability and inability

To give life unto life

Bearing the often-devastating inability to reproduce

To suffer miscarriages

And abortions

None of us anticipated

Tubal pregnancies that poison our systems and take our lives

Cesarean surgeries that expose us to near death

And natural births that put pressure on our lungs and heart

To function in less space

Moving all of our organs out of place

Carrying children that sap the marrow from our bones

Delivery

Spreading our pelvic regions to points that would break a man

You are telling me

I am not a woman

Because I didn't have the surgery

My gender is an illusion that doesn't count

Because they could

Because they were empowered to

Redefine themselves

In their eyes

A woman's struggle to get an education

To vote

To lead

To work

To participate in sports

All inconsequential

Circumstantial evidence

Not viable

The struggle women face to be heard, seen, understood

That now that you can mold the ass I was born with

Take pills to create the breast that I nursed my children on

And go under the knife to construct a functioning vagina

You dismiss mine

Though you came out of one

Now you are trying to tell me

That womanhood never existed

Until after your re-birth

Even though

Biologically and surgically

You are the afterbirth

Of my existence

The prototype of my grand design

Homophobe, transphobic

That's what you call me when I stand up for me

Changeling

You keep trying to change me

Proselytizing

Saying I hate you because I love me

This is not new

It is indeed what extremist men do

Have always done

From the beginning of time

Name things

And when they want to change things

Rename them

Disclaim them

Whatever suits their need

You, your, they, them, he, she, it, shit.

I am a woman

This is not up for discussion

They want the law to question my being

If you want to change, choose to change

To align with the dysphoria you feel

That's fine

But don't dare tell me

That I am not a woman

Because you changed your mind,

Trying to use transgenderism to get out of

Or commit

A crime

I, for one,

Will not cooperate in your fraudulent delusion.

# REMINISCE

Yesterday I watched a crack addict walk down the street where I grew up

Head bowed; overly lean body bent

His face a mass of wrinkled pain masking his youth

Dressed in all black

Black as a night without stars

Dressed in death

I felt sad

And afraid.

I sat on my momma's porch reminiscing

There are no more trees lining the street

Trees I used to climb as a gangly young girl

Playing hide and seek with my siblings and neighborhood friends

Trees I loved and admired with their strong trunks

And gnarled limbs

Raised branches lifted to the sun like hands in worship

Now

The neighbor's yard is overrun with unattended shrubbery, discarded waste,

And overgrown trees whose branches lay lazily across my mother's fence

The same yard where we used to play baseball

I never got a hit, but I could run

Boy, could I run

Now, I watch birds, squirrels, and insects gather in the weeds that have grown

In the untended tree

Its overgrowth creeping menacingly towards me

Yesterday,

I walked to the end of the street with an old friend

For the first time

I was extremely conscious of my surroundings

And not in the curious, excited way that I was as a child

The old neighborhood is still polished

The multitude of handicap signs giving witness to the age of its residents

People don't sit on their porches so much

Or leave the house other than for work and church on Sunday

I am cautious

A white man who had parked his car behind my mother's while she was away

Was killed in that spot.

Shots ring on this street now

One of the last vestiges of quiet suburban life in the city

I stand guarded and alert here

Knowing the reality of catching a sudden stray bullet

My friend stands watching too

Wary and protective.

Yesterday I sat on my mother's porch and sang

The birds gathered in the clump of trees and overgrowth next door

To sing with me

A squirrel rushed back and forth along the neighbor's fence

I sang until the neighbors on the other side came home

I sang till my spirit felt free and unencumbered

I sang of those glory days

When trees lined the street

And I climbed their gnarly limbs

To play hide and seek.

# DEAR DADDY

I used to write you letters when I was a little girl

I know you never got a single one

Because heaven doesn't have a postal service

I missed you

I had to talk to you

I'm 63 years old now and still

I miss you

Still cry for you

I try to imagine what it felt like when you laughed and played with me

Cause I only have old, cracked pictures of your smile

Everyone says you laughed a lot

Joked a lot

Loved to dance and play the piano and sing

I imagine you

Raising me up onto your shoulders

Wondering if I felt the magnitude of how broad and welcoming they were

For your little girl

I see you in your air force uniform

And your flight suit

Imagine you under the wing of an airplane

Checking the engine

And I'm proud to call you daddy


I wish I could hear your voice again

Wish I could remember what it sounds like

60 years you've been away

So far away I can't reach you, touch you, or see you

Can't even find your grave

I'm not a little girl anymore

I'm all grown up daddy

With children and grandchildren of my own

Can you see me

I miss you so much

Still.

# THE DARK PLACES

Sometimes I scream into the dark places

Nobody hears me

Nobody cares

Nobody knows

Sometimes I cry in the middle of the night

Howl into my pillow

When morning comes

The tears are dry

And I smile

So nobody sees

And nobody cares

And nobody knows.

# PARANORMAL

He was a part of me

So much a part of me that it doesn't matter

That I shredded all the pictures

Burned the letters

Deleted his face from my computer screen

Tried dating again

Six days

And in three, I realized the attraction

Tried to ignore the fact that

He held his mouth like you

Kissed like you

Touched me like you but with rougher hands

Thought and dreamed and even sang like you

But he did not have your voice or your song

So I ended it and find myself still

Looking for you

Even though I don't mean to

In another man's face

A different embrace

At the end of the day

I walked away

But my soul remains tied

Like a triple braided cord

To a shadow.

# GHOSTS

It was vivid.

The memory of him.

How warm the feel of his mouth on hers.

How he tasted like morning, noon, and night after

A cigarette smoked lazily while she curled beneath his arm.

Arms powerful and strong that held her close and gentle.

Secure.

But that then and then seemed a millennium away.

She could hardly remember his name.

The distance between them had grown so wide.

"What are you thinking?"

"Nothing"

Lies

She thought of dreams and yesterdays

The agony of remembering forming a great knotted ball in her stomach

Her throat on fire from swallowing tears.

He could not know.

Would not know.

She kept silent knowing her words didn't matter anyway.


"You are wonderful you know."

He was a handsome demon.

Full of life and energy and smiles that shone through iridescent eyes.

Creative, vibrant, and strong.

Almost the antithesis of the one in her memory.

But she did not love him.

Did not care to love him.

Love had eaten her soul leaving fear in its wake.

Fear forbade her climb upon love's beauteous wings and fly.

Wonderful?

Hmmm.

Wonder when this feeling will go away.

The numbness

The mental absence that shielded her

From the memory of one she had loved

Once upon a time.


His lips were fine and full.

His kiss hot molten fire.

Left her feeling him still long after he was gone.

Oh, gentle brother, who sits in awe of beauty unseen by others

In magnitudes only you can fathom.

Gentle spirit.

I wish you happiness and joy.

And love.

But you are not the one.

She touched his face with fingers light and kissed him

Full.

Tasted the scent of flowers and innocence and hunger.

She fed him with life and walked away.


He was not a handsome man.

His face too rugged, his features raw.

But he made her laugh.

Touch me.

No, you are not the one.

One to make my weakened spirit strong.

Build castles in the sky.

I do.

And reach them only as they become air

Slipping between my fingertips, mocking me.

No, you are not the one.


"You are special."

She knew it was a line.

Childish.

He was old enough to know that she had heard it all before.

She smiled.

His body was hard.

Solid as the walls she had erected.

But even in his gargantuan strength

He could not climb over

Build over

Or reconstruct the walls to build with her.

She looked at his hands and remembered how moments ago

He had made love to her with hands alone.

She kissed him.

Left him feeling her presence long after she had gone.


Time heals all wounds

Or so they say.

And who are they?

For her,

Time had stopped.

Baby New Year strangled to death

On Father Time's long white beard.

There she stood

Naked

Raw

Empty

In the center of eternity

Not knowing,

Insecure and incapable of understanding

She stood

Anxious

And afraid.

The royal meadow grass representing her name

Had turned to muddy, brown sod

Beneath the scorching sons

That damaged her soul.

The ghosts of her past pulling at her from behind.

The demon of what should have been

Laughing in her face.

# HEAVEN CAME FOR ME

Heaven came for me last night

I was hoping it came to take me

To see my son,

My fathers, and grandfather

My brother and uncle

To hear their many voices again

I was surprised

But unafraid.


Heaven came for me last night

In a lucid dream

Stood over my bed.

Waking me

Gently

Softly

Like a whisper

I heard its spirit speak from somewhere in my sub-conscious


Heaven came for me last night

And just left me be.


Heaven came for me last night

But it didn't take me

Rejected

I'm still here

But why

Why did it come

And go

Didn't heaven hear my tears

Feel my physical pain that was too much for me to bear

Why didn't heaven come to set me free from it all

Doesn't heaven know that I'm fatigued.


Heaven came for me last night

Did it come to comfort me in my sleep

I heard no angels singing

Felt no comforting kiss and no one held my hand

There was no light or tunnels

Just a presence

Sent for me


Heaven came for me

But it left

And I am awake

Alone

And alive.

# THROUGH MY BROTHER'S EYES

[For my baby brother, Derek Armand Jennings

November 10, 1967 to March 17, 2010]

He was my twin brother

Born six years later than I

On my birthday

I didn't appreciate him for that

Cause his arrival ruined my sixth birthday party

I had six-year-old plans

But

Through my brother's eyes

I wonder if he wondered

Who all those people were staring down at him

And why were they celebrating

His entrance into the world.


When he was nine

My siblings and I called him


"Paragraph Man"

Because he never could

Or would

Answer a question simply

"Derek, what time is it?"

His answer,

"Did you know that in Spain it's x-y-z time

And in Germany the time is…."

Twenty minutes later

Even though we had already figured out the answer

He would still be sharing his FYI

Talking long after we had all stopped listening.

Through my brother's eyes

The tiniest details were particularly important and attention to detail

Was his special genius.


It seemed he shot up from five foot nothing

To six-foot-three overnight

With knobby knees and long, always ashy, legs

Wearing his signature tiny shorts that my mother hated

With long white sweat socks with red bands at the top

And dress shoes

Most times

His attire 'bout drove my mother crazy but

Through my brother's eyes

At sixteen

He was

Sexy.


He drank tea with so much sugar it looked like maple syrup.

He ate banana twin cakes by the dozens

Loved sweets

And liked to watch the ninja turtles on television

And karate movies

With subtitles.

He loved children

They loved him back

He was as much a child himself

Through my brother's eyes

Innocence never died.


He visited the sick

Whether he knew them or not was irrelevant

When you were down

He showed up to lift you

Out of weariness with his strength

Out of suffering with his compassion

Out of bitterness with kindness, laughter, and grace

He lifted you

Out of sorrow with comfort and a listening ear

He lifted you

Out of bondage

With a strong arm

And a ready shoulder

He lifted

No matter who you were

Or what path you were on because

In my brother's eyes

We were all the same

All in need of rescue from time to time


He was as stubborn as a mule

And proud as a king

But his heart was pure gold

His favors were favors

His yea was yes and amen

Through my brother's eyes

His hands

His work,

His heart

People saw God


He was a dreamer

Dreaming big dreams

Writing visions

Making them plain with paper, pencil, pen

So he could run who read them

Weaving a tapestry of hope

For himself and the world around him

Through my brother's eyes

There was a future with promise, joy, and hope.

Through my brother's eyes

When he was too sick to speak,

When I didn't know if he could hear me

When I wasn't sure if he saw me

Or knew me

When he looked at me with a clouded gaze

Through my brother's eyes

Holding his massive hands in mine

Touching my lips to his forehead and cheeks

As he faded from me

Every day as he passed from this life

Into the newness of life

I saw life

Through my brother's eyes.


Derek showed me how important it is to live on purpose

To fulfill destiny

Without a word spoken

Even as his breath slowed and

Finally

Stopped

When he could no longer feel

Or touch

Or see

I saw,

And felt,

And learned so much

Through my brother's eyes.


We love you Derek

Forever and always

We will remember and celebrate life

Through our brother's eyes


Happy New Birth Day

Live on the other side

In love and peace.

# THERE

You were there for me

I will always remember

That you were there for me

When I was on top of the world

And when the world came crashing down

All around me

You were there for me.

And I was there for you

When life treated you kind

And when life blew your mind

Almost totaling who you were

And wanted to be

You were there for me

And I was there for you.

Big sister

Baby brother

Now you've gone away

One day

I will see you again

But today

I miss my best good friend

Who was there me

And I was there for you.

# DEATH IS DISRESPECTFUL

Death is disrespectful

But it is fair

It takes our loved ones and those we despise

With equal rigor

It has no color lines

And does not discriminate

Rich, middle class, or poor

It laughs at our social constructs of status and place.

Death is disrespectful

Coming oftentimes unbidden

The unwanted, uninvited interloper

Death is an intruder of time, space, and place.

Death is disrespectful

But it is fair

It has no regard for piety, political party, or personal agendas

A generous heart will not save

A superior mind is a waste

Death comes either way

Neither youth or wisdom can prevent its call

The meek and the malicious both die with cruel or kind descent.

With no regard for life, death is disrespectful

Erasing all that existed before its time

Leaving an empty carcass behind

Death is disrespectful, but it is fair

It is only the living then, that counts

# TODAY

Today I want to scream
And stomp my feet
Cry out loud
And alone

Today I want to punch her lights out
Hit her right in the face
See her blood on my balled-up fist
Today

Today I don't want anybody to tell me how to grieve
How I should and should not feel
The politically correct way
To express myself
Don't tell me I should forgive
Fuck!
My feelings are my own
My grief unique because it's mine

Today I want to scream
And stomp my feet like a child
Throw a temper tantrum
Roll on the floor screaming and crying

Extra loud

Alone

Today


Instead

Today

I will not answer my phone

Or interact with anyone

I won't pace the floor

I will work

And pretend

That everything is okay

So no one knows

No one discovers

How much pain I am in

Today

I will be strong

As expected.

# ANOTHER COUNTRY

I write to escape

To fly away to another country

Where someone loves me

And cares that I exist

Where I am special

And important

Not because I serve or give

But just because I am

I fly away

In my waking dreams

To another country

Another place

Where my best friends don't die

Where people remember my name

Where my brother is still my brother

Laughing with me

His fist full of banana cake and a cup of sweet tea

I write

And I fly away

# FRAGILE

Crying

I keep crying

Can't keep it together

Have to walk away from people

Look away from people

Cause I can't stop crying

Help me

Somebody

Hold me

But don't touch me

Hate people touching me

Strangers who don't know me

Acting like they do

Who didn't know him

Acting like they care

Now so concerned

But were you there

When he was sick

And my mother was alone

Now you come

You give your condolences

But you really didn't know him

And you try to touch me

Put your arm around me

Kiss my cheek

And I want to slap you

But instead

I hang on by a thread

To the manners my momma taught me

I quickly

Cleanly

Move away

From strangers

And even people I know well

Cause I don't want anybody to touch me

Too fragile

So fragile now

I just might break

Crying

# RESURRECTION

I will write myself to life

A crucifixion

And resurrection

I will write myself a living requiem


I will write myself to life

Die

Memorialized

Resurrected on a page

Once, twice, infinity

Eternally written into time


I will write myself to death

And life

Living

Dying

On repeat

I will resurrect myself more times than Jesus Christ

With this pen

On a page

I will write myself

To life

And death

And life repeatedly

# CHAPTER 7

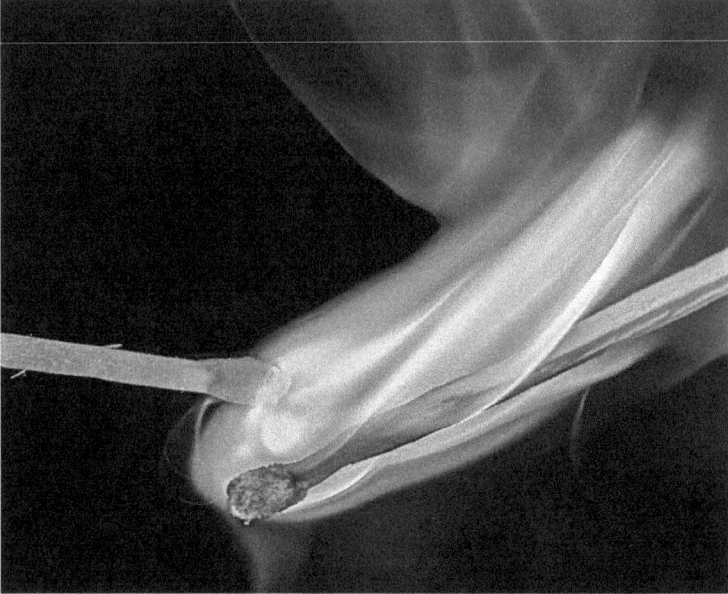

# LIGHT AND FIRE

There will be times when it will not be enough
To go through the fire.
You will have to become
The fire
And the light.

# PURIFY

It is the word that cleanses me from all unrighteousness

The words of my mouth

The meditations of my heart

The weeping that may endure

For many nights

Purifying my heart and soul.


It is the word that cleanses me

The word that heals me

The words I heard

The words I spoke

The words I've lived

It is the word that purifies my soul.

# LIGHT AND FIRE

Moses had the burning bush

I have become the fire

The ten virgins had their lamps

I have become the flame

I have lived through the darkness

And have become the light

Illuminating the path that blinds you

And the fire that warms your soul.

I have become the pillar of smoke

The cloud

Guiding you by day

The nourishing rain

The winds caress

I am the light and the fire

That shows you the way to

Fear not

I am the fire

And the flame

That now leads you through the darkness

Illuminating your days

I feed the spark, the well of life inside of me

Never be extinguished

I rise again.

# DIVINITY

Today I renew my own strength

I wait on the voice of my inner being

For guidance and direction

I wait for divine intuition

I wait for the light to dismantle the effects of darkness

Unveiling shadows

Making all things new again

I listen

And I wait

Then I mount up on invisible wings

Enlightened, expansive, powerful wings

I mount up

Not relying on the strength of the branch

I open my wings

And soar

Eagle scorpion that I am

I slice through the air

Stinging the dark clouds

Unveiling the light above them

With the intrinsic power of life and death

I mount up on wings, slicing the sky

Floating high upon the air

Resting on currents and turbulence, I mount up and soar

Waiting

For the next direction.

# VERSUS

Church folks say

"Don't let your good

Be evil spoken of."

But how can one help that if others

Are intent on speaking evil

Pretending good

I say

Let your good be evil spoken of

Let your haters hate with passion

But don't let that change who you are

Or the good that you do

Instead

Continue

With power, purpose, and passion

Cause whoever judges you

Judges themselves too

Whoever designs a noose for you

Will inevitably be hung by it too

So let your good be evil spoken of

Let your haters hate with passion

But don't let it change

The good that you do.

# SOWING AND REAPING

I came upon a field of goodness

With rows of trees and wildflowers

Trees of good and evil

Of knowledge, freedom, ease

And power.

I came upon a field of goodness

Of greens, and purples, and yellow hues

Where passersby didn't notice

Their minds filled with pacing

Intent on social media

Hearing and absorbing bad news

But there I sat or stood and listened

Staring for hours at the power of silence

In a fruitful field


I've come upon a field of goodness

The grasses grow long and green here

Flourishing beneath the sun

Standing here, I think about what I can become

I see the garden that no one knows growing, becoming beneath my feet

I see myself and what was sown inside of me

I see how much I've grown, reaching the height of one tall tree.

I am the product of this field

The field of goodness

Is me.

# MORE THAN ENOUGH

People talk about being a survivor

As if it's the greatest thing in the world

But survivor

Doesn't mean conqueror

Doesn't mean overcomer

Doesn't mean one who thrives

I have no desire to merely survive

I am

More than a conqueror

I am

A champion

I am

The head and not the tail

I am

The above only and never the beneath

I am

Ahead and not behind

I am

On time

And never too late

I am

Progressing

I am

Moving forward

I am

More than enough.

I am

I am

I am

Overcoming, outliving, outlasting my broken heart

And depressive mind

My challenging health

And capricious bank accounts

I am

Destined for more

I am

Winning

You go ahead and merely survive

I am feasting at the banquet table of the empowered overcomers

Amen.

# DRY BONES

Ezekiel had a conversation with some dry bones

His message so powerful

That flesh formed

Cells regenerated

Brain waves

Synapses connected

Muscle

And sinew

And strength

And breath of life

Entered

And those dry bones

Renewed and restored

Lived

Dead bones are not the end

There is a resurrection

When we speak life to the thing

That would have us believe

It's over.

# LOOKING GLASS

Once upon a time I looked in the mirror and didn't see myself

Didn't recognize my own face

Now they call me Queen

And I laugh

Tell them that's not news

I already know who and what I am

I never needed you to identify me

Just needed to straighten my crown

And continue.

Once upon a time I looked in the mirror and didn't like myself

You're beautiful

No matter who said it

I didn't believe it, but now

I know

You don't have to tell me that

I see me shining from the inside out

I see the sparkle in my eye that knows

How brightly I shine.

Once upon a time I looked in the mirror and questioned my existence

Asked who am I

What do I want

What am I doing here

And I received the answers

As the Spirit guided me back to myself

Once upon a time I looked in the mirror and saw an unfamiliar face

But that was once upon a long, long, time ago

When people tried to sell me their fairy tale version of me

The version that walked, talked, and acted like they wanted

The people pleasing version of me

The humiliated version of me

The broken version of me

I was unconscious

But I'm wide awake now

And the version of me that is me

The indefatigable me

The "I don't give a fuck" me

The FAFO me

The cut you with my eyes, my tongue, deeper than a knife wound me

The resilient me

The all things are possible

Because I believe in me

Has arisen

And there ain't nothing you can do about that

Thank you for your contribution

To the powerful me

That I've become.

# I AM

Who will I say that sent me

I am

He said

I am that I am

The beginning and the end

Before me there was none like me

After me there will not be another

I am

The light of the world

A fire that burns through the darkness

A candle that cannot be hidden

I am

The wellspring of life

The river inside me

Watering everything around me

Springing forth fruitful, multiplying

I am all that is and was and is to come

I am the universe

Mastery and Divinity

I am the father, mother, and the son

Eternal, I am from everlasting to everlasting

I am the alpha

Female

And the omega

Lasting one

I am

The above only

Without condescension

I am here

I am also

There

And everywhere

In you

And you in me

I have populated the world

I am she

The way

The truth

And the life giver

The wombed one

The deliverer

And healer

The redeemed and the redeemer

The restored and the resurrection

I am the life giver and the life

I am

# GRATEFUL

It feels so good to pen a word or two of my own

To write for someone else

To tell their stories

Is interesting and rewarding work

But to pen my own truth

Tell my own story

Sing my own song on a page

Is the most life affirming witness

And revelation

To who I am

And who I am becoming

I'm so grateful for this pen

So grateful for these words

So grateful for this gift.

# BELOVED

My father tells me that I am beautiful

Every day

He whispers those words to me

Every day he brings me his gifts

Gifts of sunlight

And clouds

Ocean waves

And sea foam

Elegant birds

And red-breasted robins

Bright colored cardinals

Magnificent blue jays

And black crows

Yellows, greens, and blues

In feathery hues

Flying above my head

Or walking so close by

I can reach out and touch them if I dare

If they allow it.

My father tells me I am beautiful

And I know

That my beauty is only a reflection

Of him

His love for

And confidence in me.

My father shows me I am beautiful

When I look in the mirror

And see beyond the flesh, bone, hair, teeth, eyes, and nose

And I believe him

Believe in what I see that he shows me.

Last night my father brought me rain and thunder

Hand claps and lightning from the sky

To get my attention

Look what I can do daughter

I am the magic in all your dreams

The electrical force behind all you desire

I can change the course of nature

And of life

With only a breath

Look what I can do

Your father

In heaven

Loves you

You are my reflection.

# GRAMMA

When did I drift into grandma?
None of my grandchildren call me any of the witty
Cute names my sibling sisters enjoy
Glammy
Nona
Abuela
I get grandma
Or graannnnmaaaaaa
Sung in a long, sing-song tone
Makes me feel like the matriarch
A queen
Or an old woman depending
My Asian Black grandson
Malachi
Was as much my baby as his mamas while she was in the military
He startles me now
The baritone in his voice
Always taking me by surprise
My eldest granddaughter has my eldest son's stoic look and piercing eyes
With beauty that transcends her name
Skye
My Puerto Rican Black babies
Sa'Ryah and Robyn Aliyah
Say Gremma with my name at the end
As if it were one word
Lyrical
My Indigenous Black granddaughter
Better known as Chocolate Bear
At 13, always asks me to rate "the fit"
Her language is always new to me
And I constantly need someone to interpret
Her brother Prince
AKA "The old man"
(even though he's only 8)
Is the keeper of the remote at my house
After a long day of school
From which he trudges in like an old man

After a hard day's work
Throws off his jacket
Kicks off his shoes
And sighs
As he falls into the couch or my chaise
Then flips on the television
With all of that, he still tries to jump into my arms for a hug
Usually stepping on my feet
No matter how careful he tries not to
Legacy,
My youngest granddaughter
My brown sugar baby
Sings the title grandma as she waltzes through the door
Cause Legacy is always the queen and never treads lightly
Softly, or unnoticed anywhere
She carries the truth of her name
And knows it.
Ny'briel, at five, teaches me from his extensive knowledge of planets
Making me realize
I am not smarter than a kindergartener
Messiah teaches me to smile
And, at barely two, shows me how to give an effective side-eye
Syre, in my presence, commands himself like a king
Opening doors for me
Carrying my groceries
And taking out the trash
Without being asked.
Ten in all
Calling me grandma
In their own unique ways
They are my legacy
My next generation of love
Their existence
Gives me new life
And for that
I am grateful.

# LEGACY

I used to write to speak only to myself
Then I shared it with others
But now as I write
I feel an urgency to leave something of myself
To leave something of my soul behind
Something that remains with my children
My grandchildren
And scores of others who I'm supposed to reach in the world
Long after I am gone
Something they can point to and say
She was here
She made a difference
She opened a door
Led a revolution
Started a movement
She was here
And
She lived.

# PHOTO CREDITS

# ABOUT THE AUTHOR

K. J. Sharpe was born and raised in Chester, Pennsylvania. Losing her father as a toddler impacted her life deeply. Extremely shy and introverted, she began to voice her thoughts and prayers in writing as early as five years old. She won her first writing competition at age six when, unknown to her, a first-grade teacher submitted her class assignment to a local poetry contest. The same happened in sixth grade when another teacher submitted a class assignment for a short speech to an oratorical contest which KJ won on several levels despite her extreme shyness. Reading has always been her favorite pastime. In high school, she volunteered to work in the library. Inspired by her high school English teacher, Mrs. Harris, KJ began submitting her work to magazines for publication. She continued to win awards for writing, oratory, and service throughout her lifetime. *Naked Screaming*, her second published work of poetry and prose, deals with the impact of complicated grief and the power of redemptive love. Her other published works include fiction novel *Love Like Rain*, self-help devotional *Broken and Spilled Out-An Abuse Recovery Journal-Recovering Yourself*, poetry, and prose *Sistah, Can You Feel Me*, and theatre scripts *CRAZY*, and *The Bride*. She can also be found on YouTube at Sharpe Turns sharing her *Turning Points* videos.

www.ingramcontent.com/pod-product-compliance
Lightning Source LLC
Chambersburg PA
CBHW060759110426
42739CB00032BA/1983